THOMAS KINKADE

Friends for Life

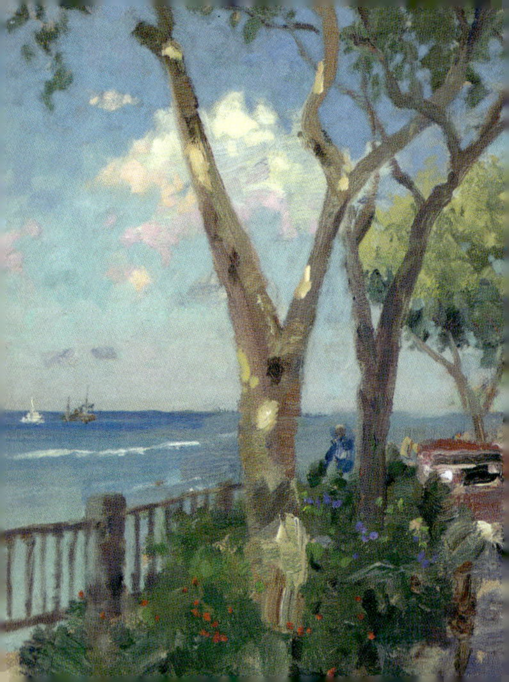

THOMAS KINKADE

Friends for Life

Andrews McMeel
Publishing

Kansas City

 For information, write Andrews McMeel Publishing, an Andrews McMeel Universal company, 4520 Main Street, Kansas City, Missouri 64111.

ISBN: 0-7407-2132-1

Library of Congress Catalog Number: 2001092775

Compiled by Patrick Regan

This book is dedicated to all the dear friends that shed their light on our lives.

In life, as in art, the presence of light makes the ordinary . . . extraordinary. And nothing sheds light on our lives like those people we call friends.

The light of friendship illuminates our daily lives and reflects back upon those loving friends who bestow it. Like light, friendship brings warmth and security to our lives. With friends, we know that we are not alone in this world . . . that there is someone *to lean on when times are difficult and someone to share in celebrating the joy and blessings that we receive.*

There is no blessing quite like a friend for life. These are the people with whom we can always be ourselves, with whom we can always share our deepest fears, our most sincere thoughts, our fondest dreams. And often, the closest of friends–like a painting–can speak volumes with no words at all.

I shall pass
through this world but once.
Any good, therefore, that I can do,
or any kindness that I can show
to any human being,
let me do it now.
Let me not defer or neglect it,
for I shall not pass this way again.

—Stephen Grellat

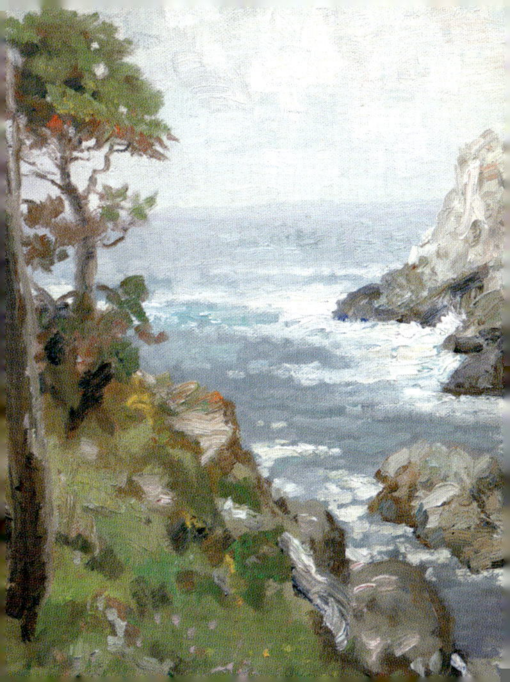

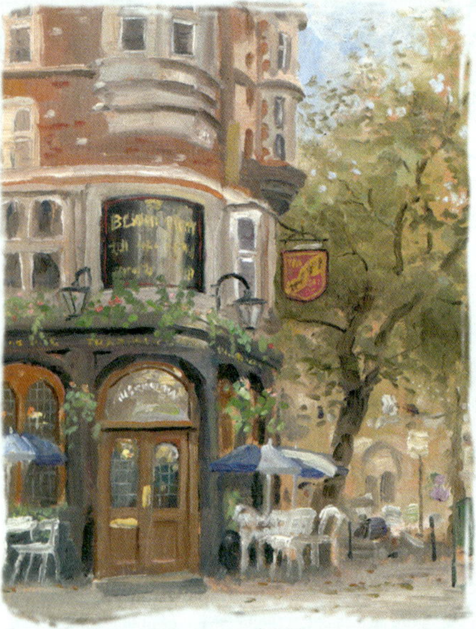

Surround yourself

with the kinds of input

that are uplifting,

that expand your mind

and settle your spirit.

—Thomas Kinkade

True happiness consists not in the multitude of friends, but in their worth and choice.

—Samuel Johnson

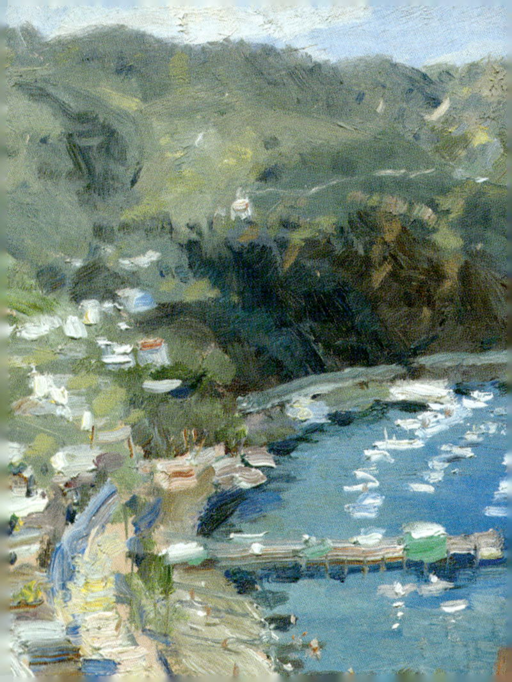

Wherever you are,
it is your friends
who make your world.

—William James

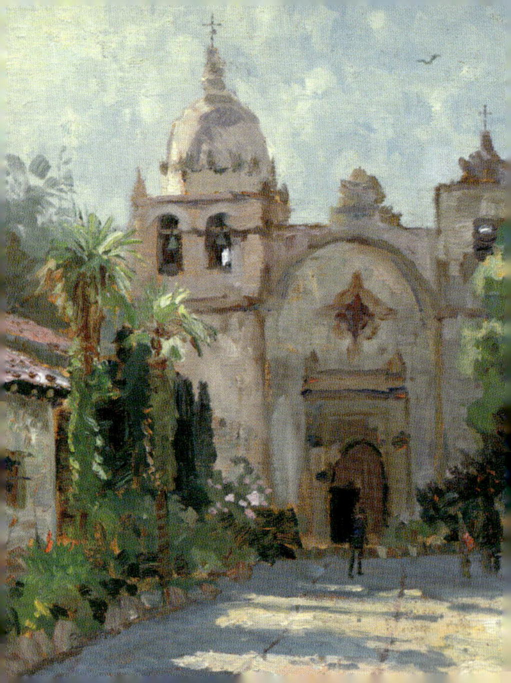

Two are better than one;

because they have

a good reward for their labour.

For if they fall,

the one will lift up his fellow:

but woe to him that is alone

when he falleth;

for he hath not another

to help him up.

—Ecclesiastes 4:9-10

If you judge people,
you have no time to love them.

—Mother Teresa

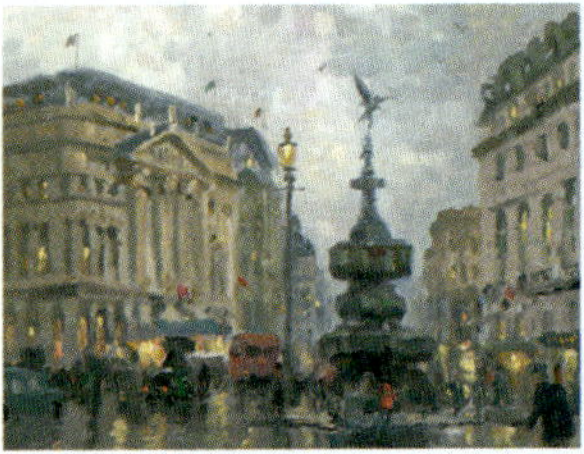

Each life has the ability

to touch other lives,

which in turn touch yet more lives.

And so, person by person,

generation by generation,

a world and a future are shaped.

—Thomas Kinkade

Arise, and get thee forth,

and seek a friendship

for the years to come.

—Alfred, Lord Tennyson

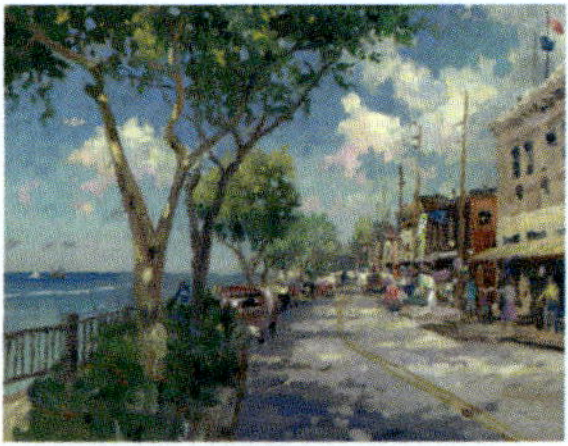

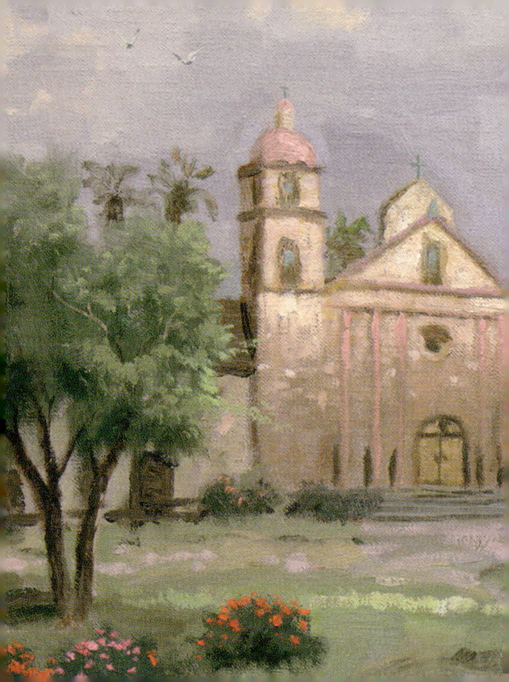

Friendship is the marriage of the soul.

—Voltaire

We are,
each of us angels
with only one wing;
and we can only fly
by embracing one another.

—Luciano de Crescenzo

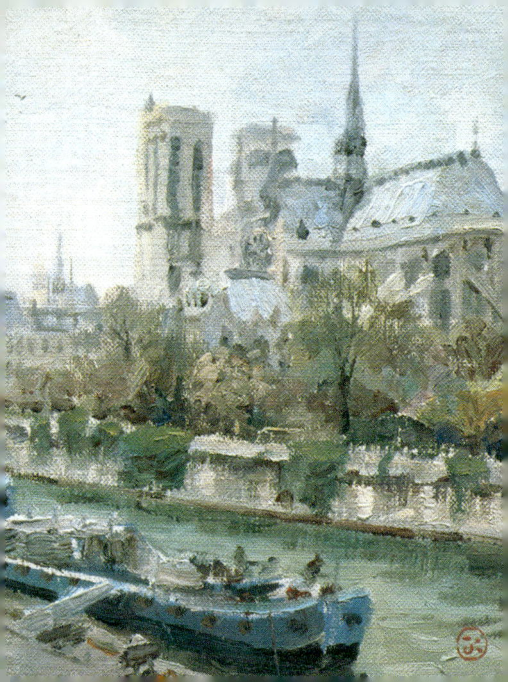

They may forget
what you said,
but they will never forget
how you made them feel.

—Carl W. Buechner

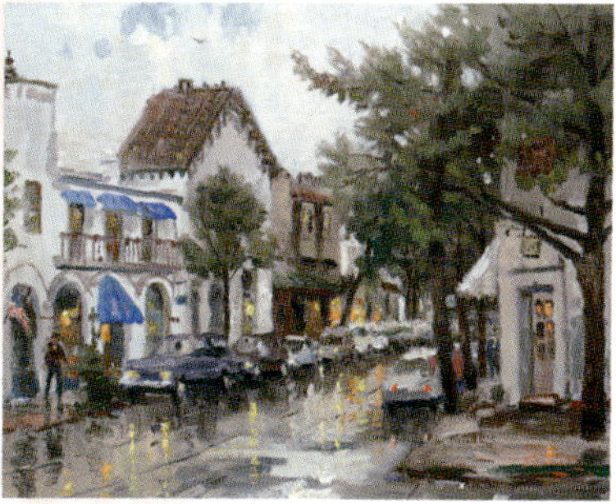

What is a friend?
A single soul
dwelling in two bodies.

—Aristotle

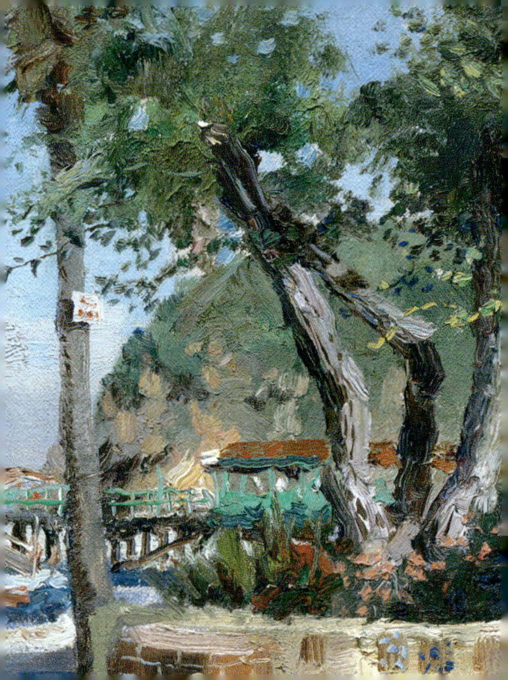

Happy is the house that shelters a friend.

—Ralph Waldo Emerson

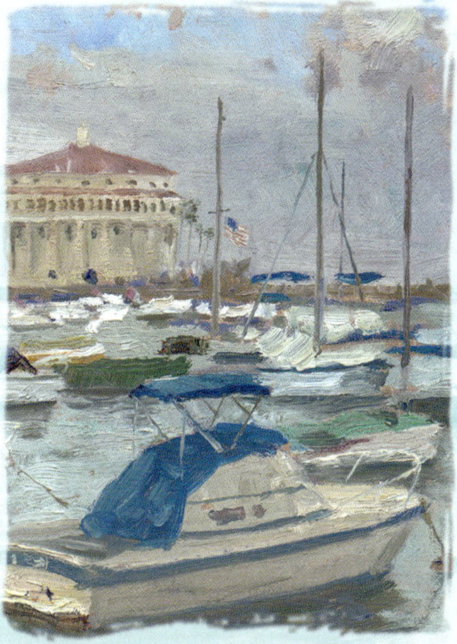

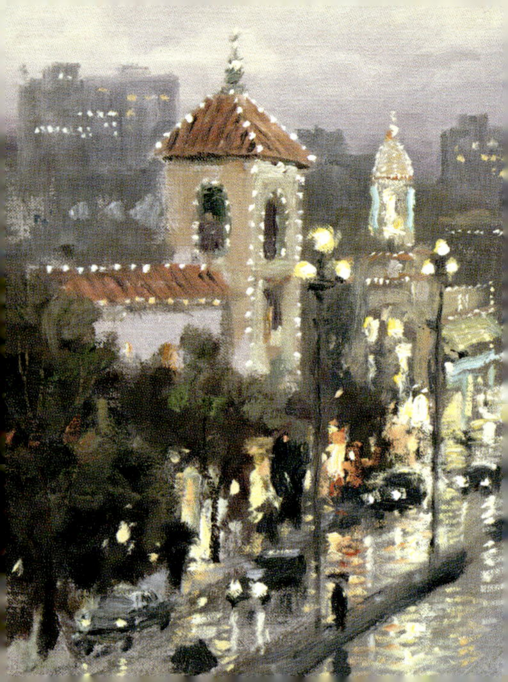

A little Consideration,
a little Thought for Others,
makes all the difference.

—A. A. Milne

Old friends are best.
King James used to call
for his old shoes;
they were easiest for his feet.

—John Selden

Friendship improves
happiness
and abates misery,
by the doubling of our joy
and the dividing
of our grief.

—Cicero

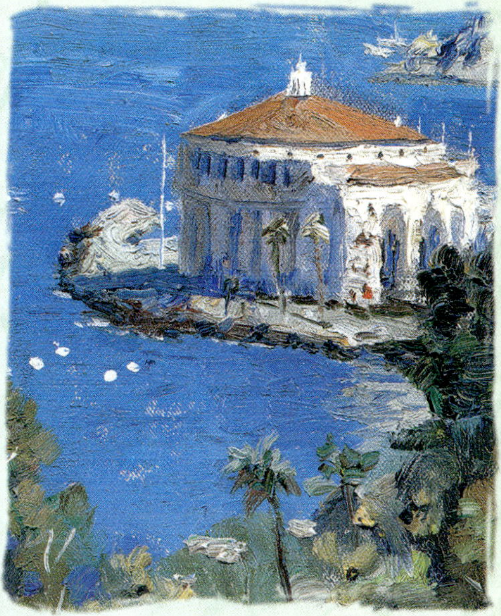

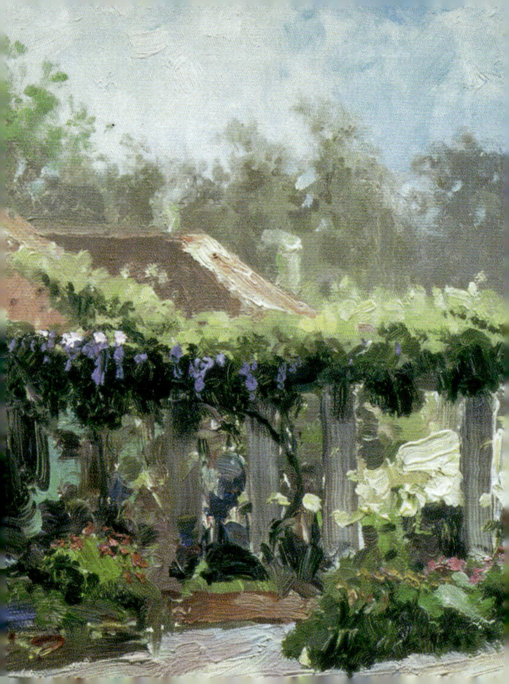

*What do we live for,
if not to make life
less difficult for each other?*

—George Eliot

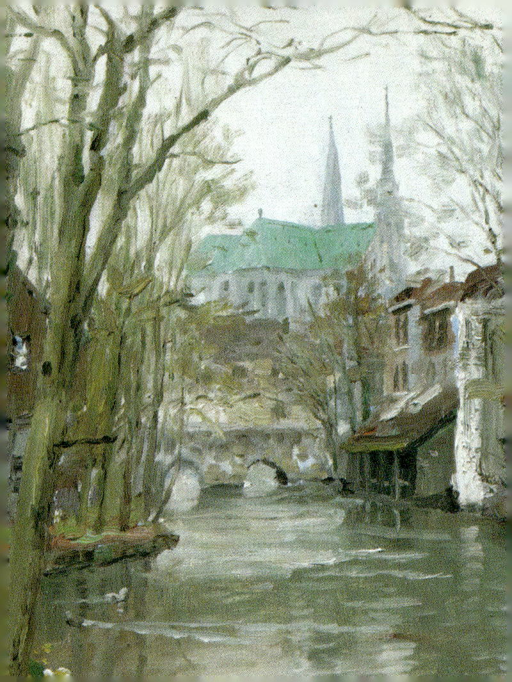

Then come the wild weather,

come sleet or come snow,

we will stand by each other,

however it blow.

—Simon Dach

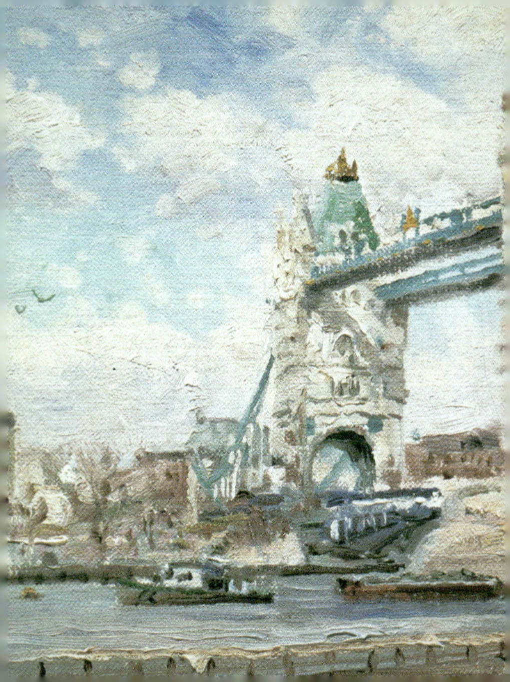

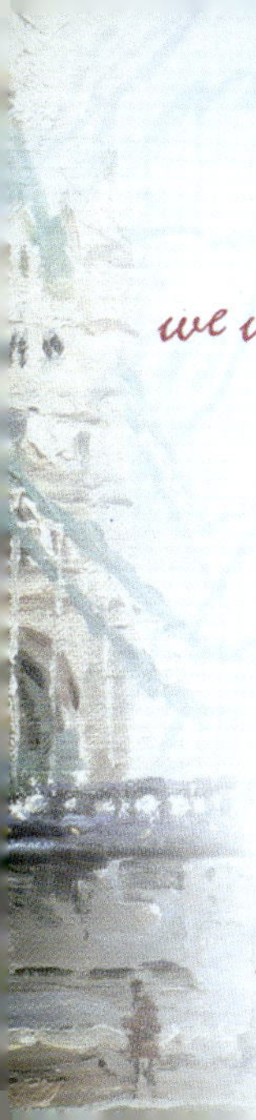

In the end,
we will remember
not the words
of our enemies,
but the silence
of our friends.

—Martin Luther King, Jr.

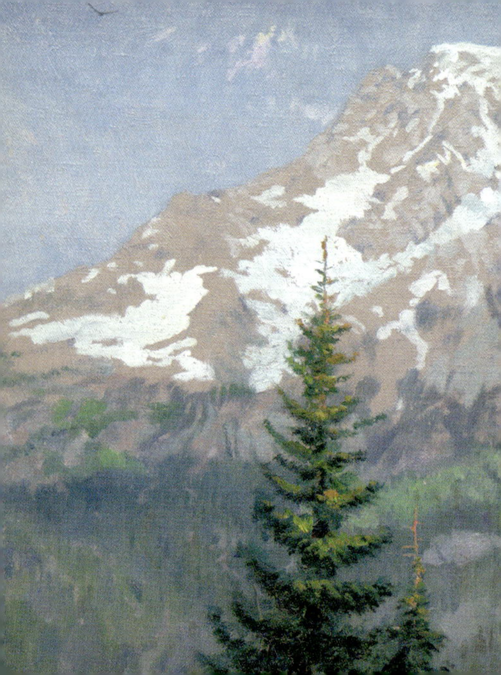

The world is so empty if one thinks only of mountains, rivers, and cities; but to know someone here and there who thinks and feels with us, and who, though distant, is close to us in spirit, this makes the earth an inhabited garden.

—Goethe

Fate
chooses our relatives,
we choose
our friends.

—Jacques Delille

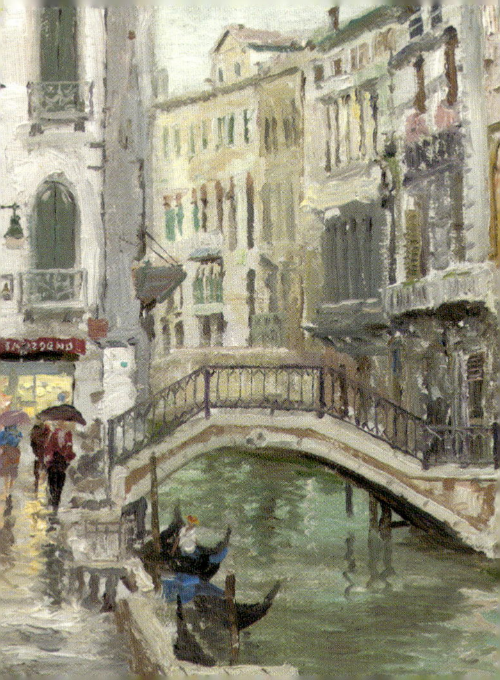

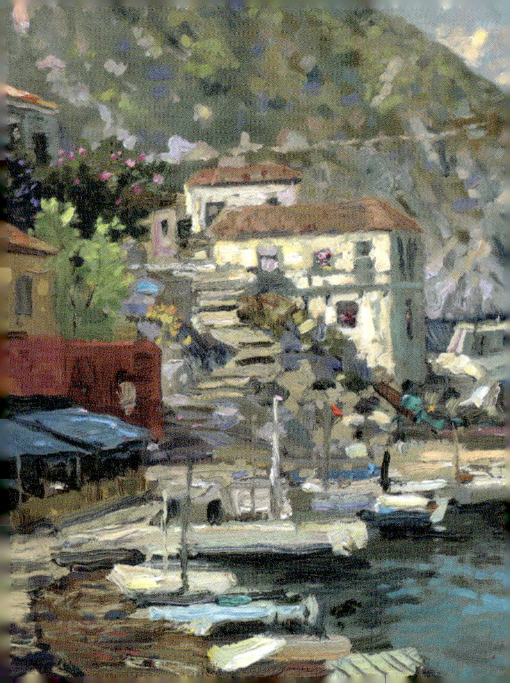

A friend

may well be reckoned

the masterpiece

of nature.

—Ralph Waldo Emerson

Let me live
in my house
by the side
of the road
And be a
friend to man.

—Sam Walter Foss

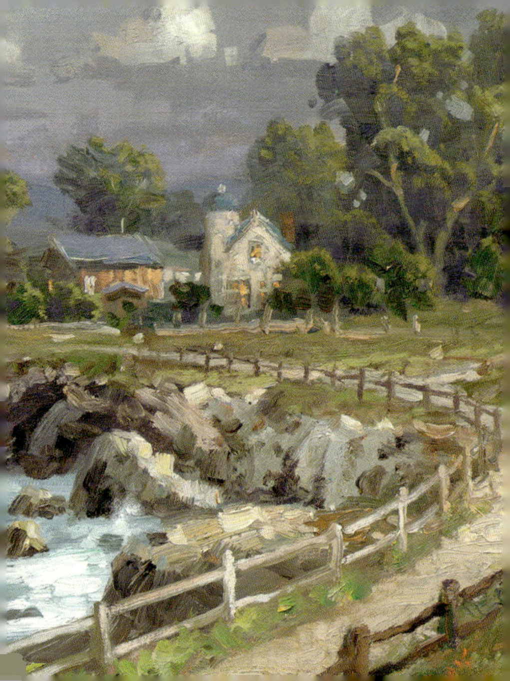

PARIS

Friendship is the golden thread that ties the hearts of all the world.

—John Evelyn

Wishing to be friends

is quick work,

friends

friendship

but friendship
is a slow ripening fruit.

—Aristotle

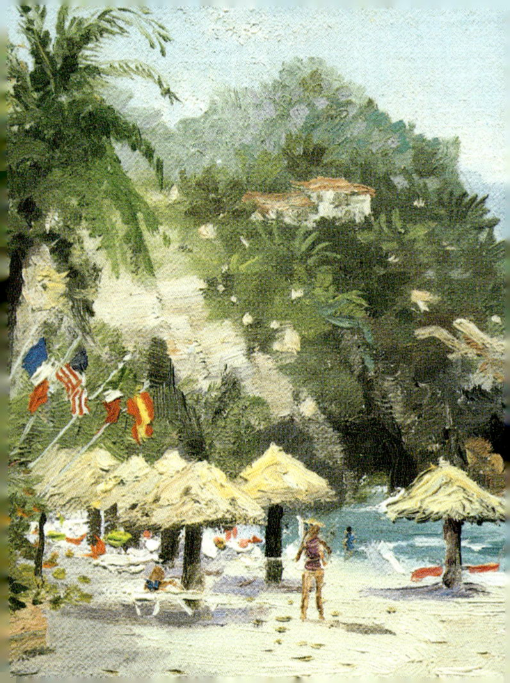

Blessed

is the influence

of one true,

loving human soul

on another.

—George Eliot

Two may talk together
under the same roof
for many years,
yet never really meet;
and two others
at first speech
are old friends.

—Mary Catherwood

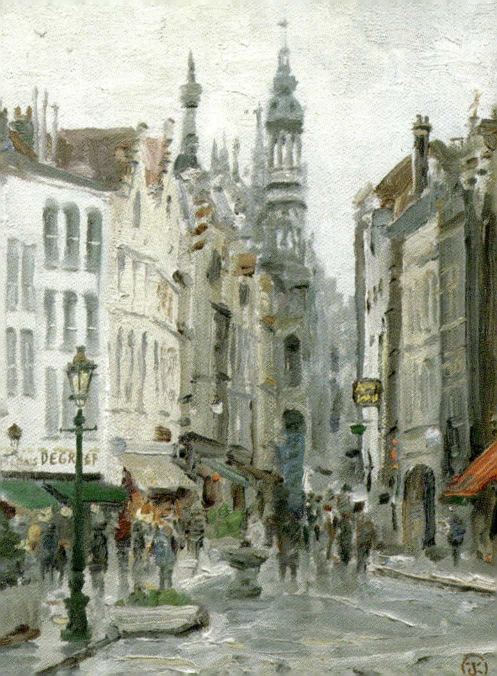

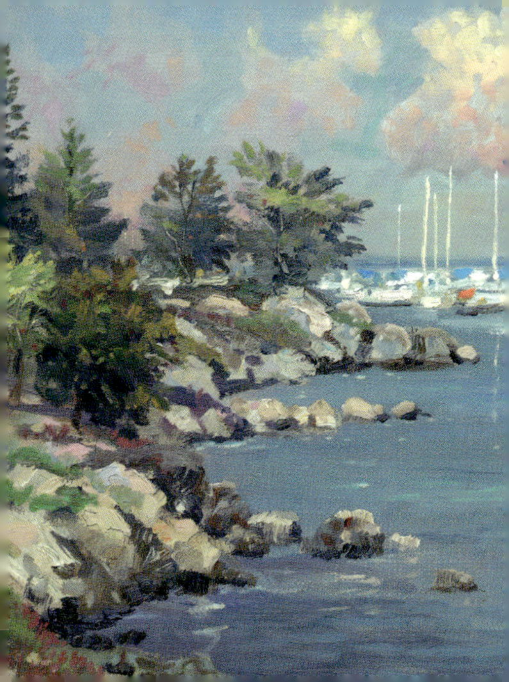

If instead of a gem,
or even a flower,
we should cast the gift
of a loving thought
into the heart of a friend,
that would be giving
as the angels give.

—George Macdonald

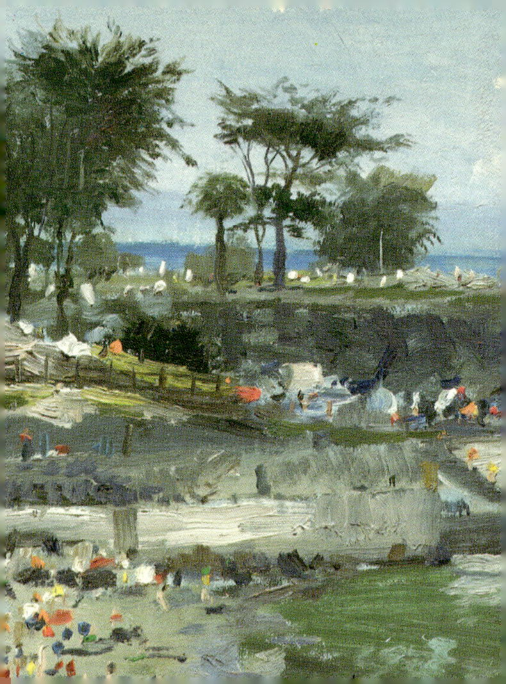

Let us be grateful
to people
who make us happy;
they are
the charming gardeners
who make
our souls blossom.

—Marcel Proust

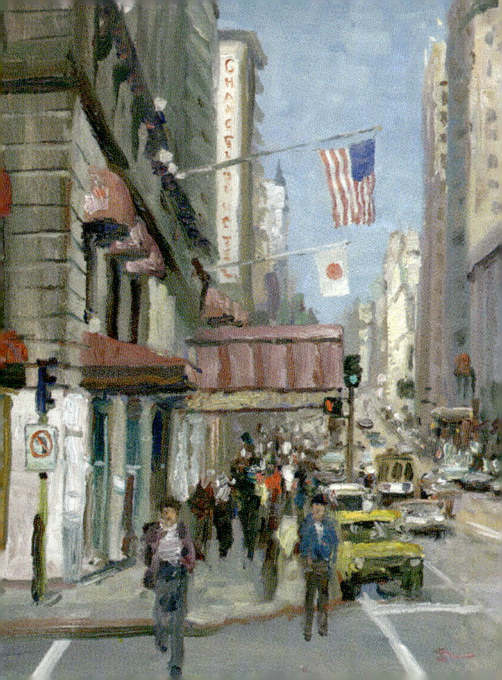

We cannot tell
the precise moment
when friendship is formed.
As in filling a vessel
drop by drop,
there is at last a drop
which makes it run over;
so in a series of kindnesses
there is at last one which
makes the heart run over.

—James Boswell

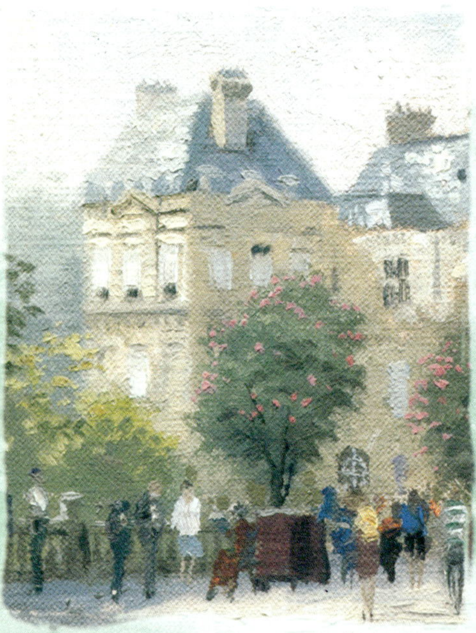

The best mirror is an old friend.

— George Herbert

The only reward
of virtue
is virtue;
the only way
to have a friend
is to be one.

—Ralph Waldo Emerson

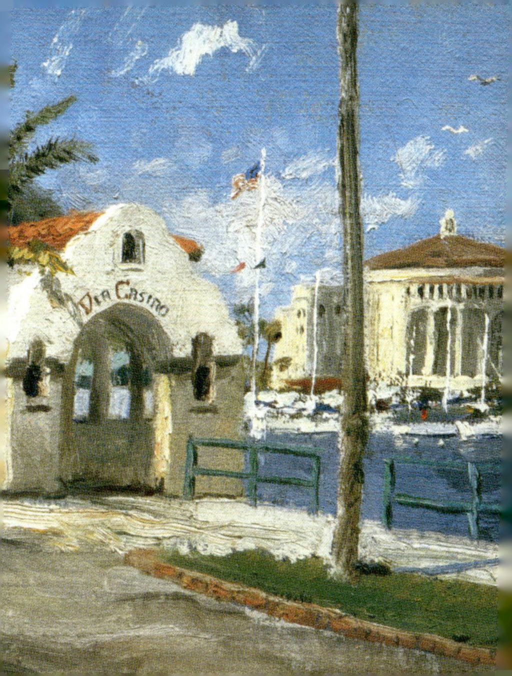
Via Casino

What greater thing is there
for two human souls
than to feel that they are joined . . .
to strengthen each other . . .
to be one with each other
in silent
unspeakable memories.

— George Eliot

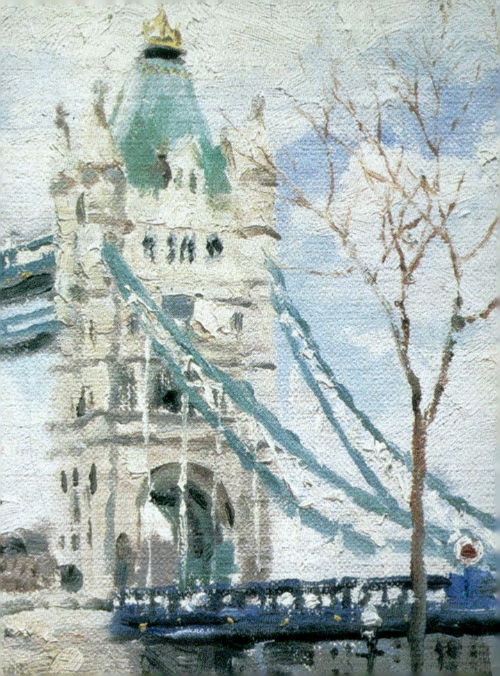

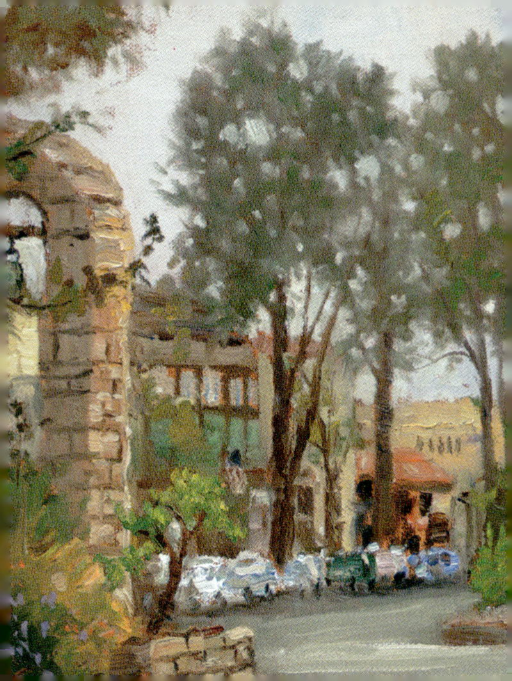

Those friends thou hast,
and their adoption tried,
Grapple them to thy soul
with hoops of steel.

— William Shakespeare

Thus nature has no love
for solitude,
and always leans, as it were,
on some support;
and the sweetest support
is found in the most
intimate friendship.

— Cicero

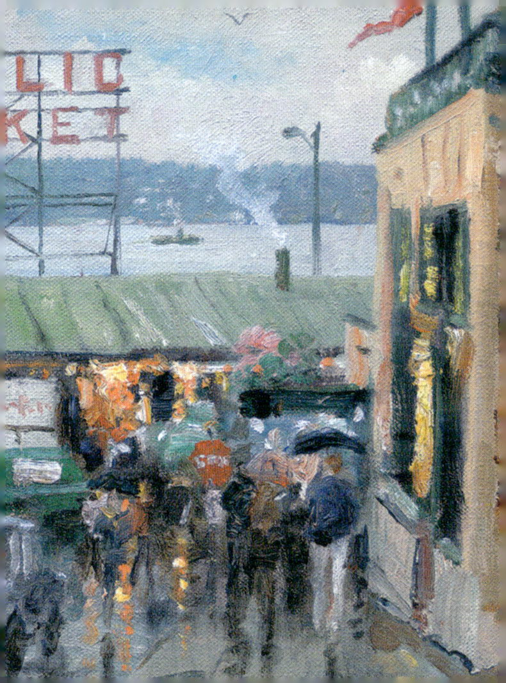
LIC
KET

Too late we learn,
a man must hold his friend
Unjudged,
accepted,
trusted to the end.

—John Boyle O'Reilly

The making of friends,
who are real friends,
is the best token we have
of a man's success in life.

— Edward Everett Hale

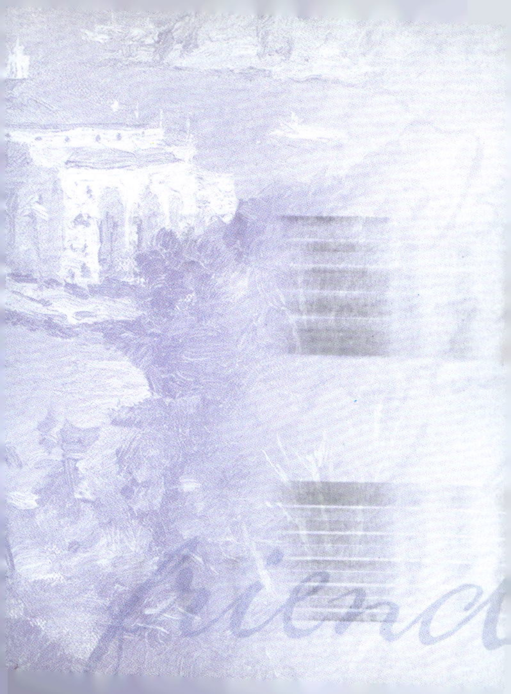